Chinese
New Year

Festivals Around the World

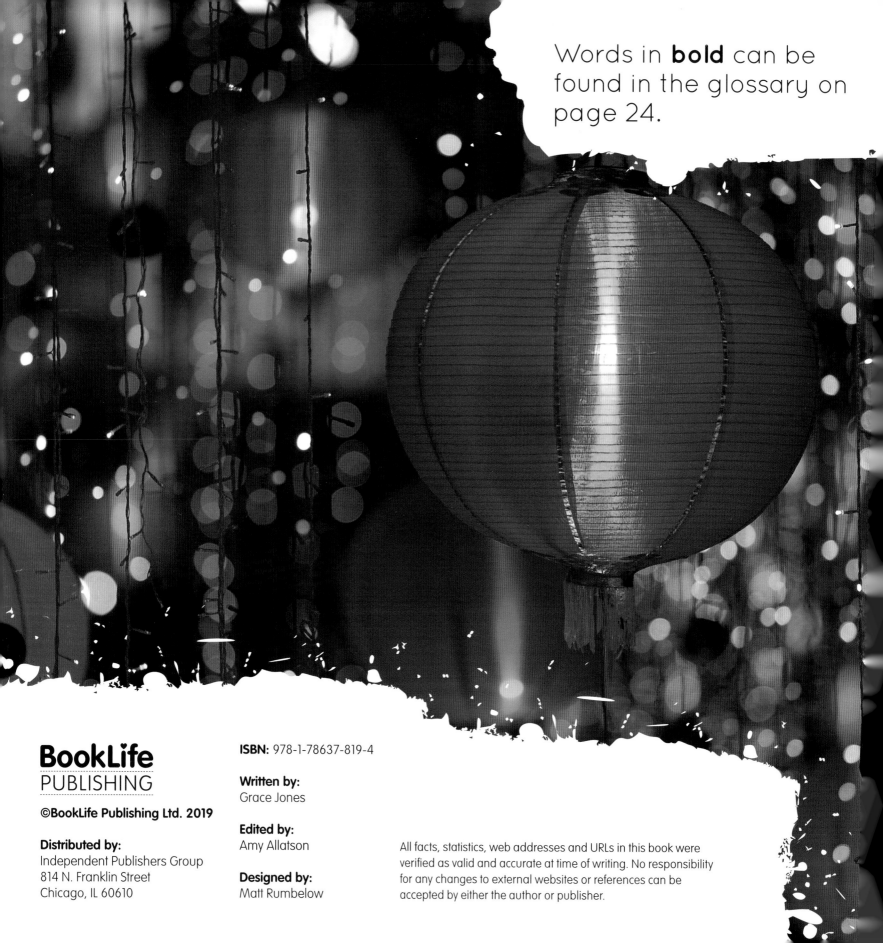

Words in **bold** can be found in the glossary on page 24.

BookLife
PUBLISHING

©BookLife Publishing Ltd. 2019

Distributed by:
Independent Publishers Group
814 N. Franklin Street
Chicago, IL 60610

ISBN: 978-1-78637-819-4

Written by:
Grace Jones

Edited by:
Amy Allatson

Designed by:
Matt Rumbelow

Some people celebrate festivals by having a party with their family and friends. Others celebrate by holding special events, performing dances or playing music.

What Is Chinese New Year?

Chinese New Year is sometimes called the Spring Festival. It happens in January or February and is mostly celebrated in China. Chinese people come together with their family and friends and celebrate the start of the new year.

Dragon and lion dances are performed during Chinese New Year.

To celebrate this special time of year, Chinese people eat festive foods, set off loud fireworks and perform **traditional** dances. Chinese New Year celebrations can last for many days.

The Story of
Chinese New Year

A long, long time ago, there was a monster named Nian who lived in the mountains. Every year the terrible monster came down from the mountains and into the small village below.

The villagers were very scared of Nian because he ate all of their animals and tried to hurt their children. Every time Nian came down from the mountains, they hid in their houses to keep their children safe from harm.

One year, a wise old man came to the village. The villagers told him how Nian scared them. The wise old man protected the village for three nights until he had to leave. Before he left, he gave them some advice. "The monster is scared by the color red and loud noises," he told them.

The next night, the villagers decorated their houses in red, made loud noises and set off fireworks to scare Nian away. Nian never came back to the village again and they were finally safe from the monster.

Family and Friends

Chinese New Year is a time when people come together to celebrate the new year with their family and friends. For many people it is the first time they've seen their family in a year.

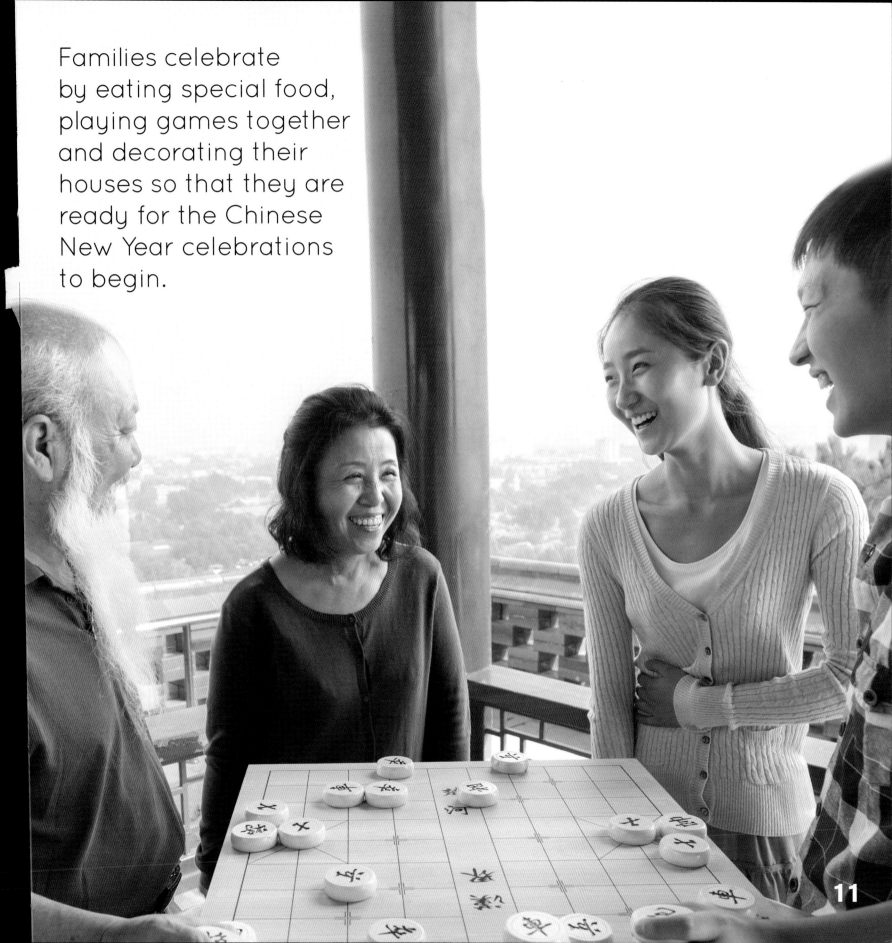

Families celebrate by eating special food, playing games together and decorating their houses so that they are ready for the Chinese New Year celebrations to begin.

11

Festive Food

All the family come together on New Year's Eve to enjoy a festive feast called Nian Ye Fan. Special dumplings filled with meat or vegetables are eaten after midnight. These are called jiaozi.

Jiaozi

Bao-Zhi says:
NEE-AN YEE FAN (Nian Ye Fan)
JY-AYE-AZ-I (Jiaozi)

Cakes, cookies and candy are eaten during the festival too. A traditional cake called **nian gao** is eaten at Chinese New Year. It is made from rice flour, water and sugar.

Bao-Zhi says:
NEE-AN GOW (Nian Gao)

Nian gao

13

Gifts

Children are given gifts of special red envelopes from their parents and grandparents. The envelopes have money inside them and are seen as lucky.

Red envelopes

Bao-Zhi says:
SHIN NEE-AN KWAI LE **(Xin Nian Kuai Le)** means Happy New Year in Chinese!

Mandarin oranges

Other gifts, such as mandarin oranges, chocolate and candles, are also given between friends and families to celebrate the start of the new year.

Decorations and Firecrackers

Red lanterns

Chinese people wear red clothes, paint their doors red and use **red lanterns** to decorate their homes. This is because the color red is thought to bring good luck.

The color red and loud noises scared Nian the monster away from the villagers.

People put **firecrackers** covered in red paper outside their houses too. When they are lit, they make a loud banging noise. Both the color red and loud noises are thought to scare away evil spirits.

The Lantern Festival

On the last day of Chinese New Year there is a big celebration called the Lantern Festival. People decorate their homes and come out onto the streets with thousands of red paper lanterns.

Red lanterns are believed to bring good luck and happiness.

People fill the streets and enjoy the music, parades, acrobats and special dances that the Lantern Festival has to offer.

Bao-Zhi says:
ZHU NEE HOW YUN (Zhu Ni Hao Yun) means 'good luck' in Chinese.

The Dragon Dance

The dragon dance is one of the many dances performed during the Lantern Festival. The tradition of dragon making began hundreds of years ago. They are usually made from paper, silk and bamboo and can take many months to finish.

Dragon dance

The dragon is held up by many performers who move its head and body so it looks like it is dancing. The dragon dance is performed to scare away evil spirits and bring good luck in the new year.

Dragons used in the dragon dance can be over 320 feet long.

21

What Year Is It?

There are 12 years in the Chinese calender that link to the 12 Chinese zodiac signs. Each zodiac sign is named after an animal. The year you were born in is your zodiac sign.

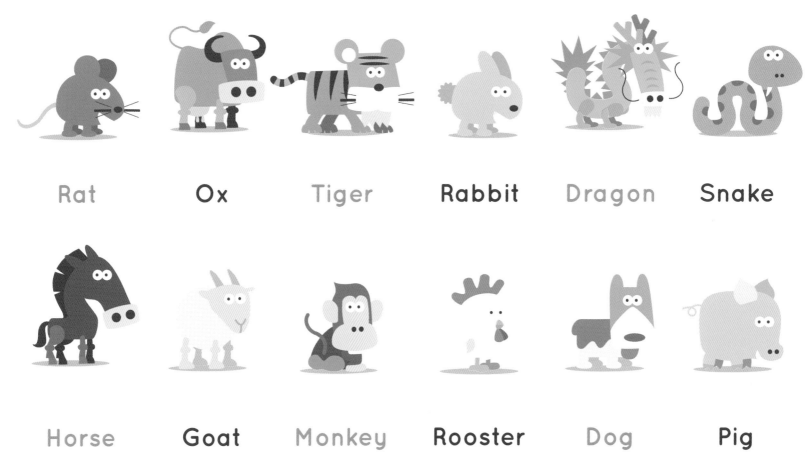

| Rat | **Ox** | Tiger | **Rabbit** | Dragon | **Snake** |

| Horse | **Goat** | Monkey | **Rooster** | Dog | **Pig** |

Each sign stands for something different. For example, people born in the year of the rabbit are said to be kind and loving. Ask an adult to help you find out which animal year you were born in.

Bao-Zhi Says...

Jiaozi
JY-AYE-AZ-I
Dumplings filled with meat or vegetables

Nian Gao
NEE-AN GOW
A traditional cake made from rice flour, water and sugar

Nian Ye Fan
NEE-AN YEE FAN
A New Year's Eve feast

Xin Nian Kuai Le
SHIN NEE-AN KWAI LE
Xin Nian Kuai Le means 'Happy New Year' in Chinese

Zhu Ni Hao Yun
ZHU NEE HOW YUN
Zhu Ni Hao Yun means 'good luck' in Chinese

Glossary

firecrackers loud fireworks

red lanterns lights covered in ball made of red paper

traditional something that is passed from person to person over a long time

Index

Credits

Photocredits: Abbreviations: l-left, r-right, b-bottom, t-top, c-center, m-middle.
Front Cover — L; Tom Wang R; tuthelens, 1L – Tom Wang, 1R – tuthelens, 2 – beltsázar, 4 – Tom Wang, 5 – Dragon Images, 7 – Dragon Images, 8 – Napatsan Puakpong, 8inset – leungchopan, 9 – manzrussali, 9inset – Sean Pavone, 10 – Dragon Images, 11 –XiXinXing, 12 – JIANG HONGYAN, 13 – aaekung, 14 – fotohunter, 15 – design56, 16 subin pumsom, 17 – cowardlion, 18 – 229394104, 19 – Rawpixel, 20 – Rawpixel, 21 – John Bill.
Images are courtesy of Shutterstock.com. With thanks to Getty Images, Thinkstock Photo and iStockphoto.

Chinese New Year

Festivals Around the World

Hello, my name is Bao-Zhi.

When you see Bao-Zhi, he will tell you how to say a word.

What Is a Festival?

A festival takes place when people come together to celebrate a special event or time of the year. Some festivals last for only one day and others go on for many months.